W9-DIL-193

FRONTIER LAND

WOMEN

OF THE FRONTIER

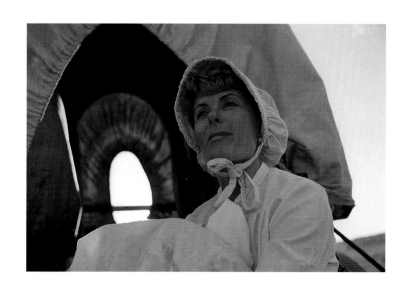

Charles W. Sundling

Visit us at
www.abdopub.com

Published by ABDO Publishing Company, 4940 Viking Drive, Edina, MN 55435.
Copyright ©2000 by Abdo Consulting Group, Inc. International copyrights
reserved in all countries. No part of this book may be reproduced in any form
without written permission from the publisher.

Printed in the United States.

Edited by: Tamara L. Britton
Art Direction: John Hamilton

Cover photo: Archive Photos
Interior photos: Corbis-Bettmann, pages 1, 3, 6-12, 15-17, 21, 23-25, 27
             Digital Stock, page 5
             Corel Corporation, page 14

Sources: *American Heritage History of the Great West, The*. New York: American Heritage, 1965; Brown, Dee. *The Gentle Tamers: Women of the Old West*.
New York: Bantam Books, 1974; Dick, Everett. *The Sod House Frontier*. New
York: Johnsen, 1954; Encarta 98 Desk Encyclopedia, 1996-97, Microsoft Corpo-
ration, 1996; Encyclopedia Britannica, Chicago: Encyclopedia Britannica, Inc.,
1993; Grolier Multimedia Encyclopedia, The 1995, Grolier Electronic Publishing, 1995; Horan, James D. *Women of the West*. New York: Bonanza Books,
1952; Jeffrey, Julie Joy. *Frontier Women: The Trans-Mississippi West 1840-
1880*. New York: Wang and Hill, 1979; Lamar, Howard (editor). *The Reader's
Encyclopedia of the Old West*. New York, 1977; Milner, Clyde A. et. al. (editors).
The Oxford History of the American West. New York, 1990.

Library of Congress Cataloging–in–Publication Data

Sundling, Charles W.
    Women of the frontier / Charles W. Sundling
        p. cm. — (Frontier land)
    Includes index.
    Summary: Describes the experiences of women who went west in the latter
part of the nineteenth century.
    ISBN 1-57765-046-8
    1. Women pioneers—West (U.S.)—History—Juvenile literature. 2. Women
pioneers—West (U.S.)—Social life and customs—Juvenile literature. 3. Frontier
and pioneer life—West (U.S.)—Juvenile literature. 4. West (U.S.)—Social life and
customs—Juvenile literature. [1. Women pioneers. 2. Frontier and pioneer life—
West (U.S.) 3. West (U.S.)—Social life and customs.] I. Title. II. Series: Sundling,
Charles W. Frontier land.
F596.S934 2000
978'.0082—DC21   98-12688
                                                          CIP
                                                          AC

CONTENTS

This young girl is wearing an outfit like those worn by pioneer girls.

WOMEN PIONEERS

In the 1840s, very few women went west. In 1841, one of the largest wagon trains going to the Pacific Coast had only one woman on it. Three years later two women went with another large wagon train to California. However, by the end of the 1850s thousands of women had gone to the new land. By 1900, 800,000 women were recorded as living west of the Mississippi River. Many women went west with their husbands. Some went with their fathers, while others went on their own.

Women went west because, like everybody else, they were looking for better lives for themselves. It was hard because many women did not want to leave their safe homes in the East. They knew the trip west would be dangerous.

Both men and women were afraid of Native Americans attacking their wagon trains. They also feared the possibility of Native American warriors kidnapping the pioneer women. When warriors attacked, they usually hurt both men and women from the wagon trains.

However, in reality kidnapping was not likely to happen. Thousands of women went west, and only a small number saw their wagon trains attacked. A smaller number of those were kidnapped. Disease, rather than Native Americans, hurt or killed more pioneers. Measles, cholera, and smallpox infected many people. In 1849, cholera killed 5,000 people on wagon trains. Many died after being sick for only one day.

A pioneer woman heads west as part of a wagon train.

Injuries also plagued the pioneers. Accidents seemed to happen every day on a wagon train. Both men and women worked with dangerous things, like axes and knives. Sometimes pioneers suffered broken arms and legs. Cooking on open fires resulted in burned fingers. During the long winters, frostbitten ears and noses were common.

Moving frightened many women, yet they moved anyway. They left their homes and went west in search of better lives.

Pioneer women feared being kidnapped by Native Americans, but accidents and sickness took many more lives than war parties.

Pioneers head west in Conestoga wagons.

MOVING WEST

Most women moved west in covered wagons, although some traveled in old farm wagons. Heavier wagons were stronger and did not break down as often. They also could travel for many miles. Conestoga was a common brand of these heavier wagons, which were often pulled by teams of oxen. "Prairie schooner" was a common nickname for the heavier wagons. A schooner is a kind of boat, and from a distance the wagon's white canvas top resembled a boat sail.

A woman on a wagon train had the same duties she had in her home. However, she had to do them under harder conditions. She had to cook meals, mend and wash clothes, and also take care of the children through rain, extreme heat, blowing wind, and sometimes snow.

Cooking food was a difficult task. Wood-burning stoves were difficult to use outside. Also, wood was difficult to find in some areas of the West, like the Great Plains. Most women learned to cook food on open fires, sometimes using buffalo chips or dried weeds for fuel. Women and children collected fuel for the cooking fire.

Many people took rice on their western trip. Rice was easy to store and did not spoil easily. Many people also took dried fruit with them, especially apples. People ate dried fruit often because the vitamins in dried fruit helped to keep the travelers from becoming sick.

Washing clothes was another difficulty. Most of the stops that a wagon train made lasted only one night. Washed clothes usually would not dry in that short time. Also, the large amount of water needed to wash clothes was often difficult to find. Heating that much water was also a problem.

Women also took care of babies and children. Women wanted to wash their children often. However, they had trouble finding water they could use. Alkali water was often the only water to be found. Alkali water stung the skin of adults and could blister a baby's skin.

A woman dressed as a pioneer throws water from a bowl onto a grassy hill while on a covered wagon vacation tour of the Oregon Trail.

A woman cooks at a chuck wagon on a tour of the Oregon Trail near Bayard, Nebraska. On the tour vacationers have a chance to simulate the pioneer experience.

Pioneers reenacting a wagon train journey cross grasslands by covered wagon and on foot.

Most of the time women and children rode in the wagons. But sometimes the wagon trails were rough, and then they had to walk. Mothers carried their babies, often for hours. Many times wives and daughters did the same work their husbands or fathers did. They hitched oxen to wagons and drove them. Now and then they had to put horseshoes on the oxen and horses.

Women on wagon trains wore clothes that protected them from the sun and wind, like bonnets and long skirts. They had boots like the ones that men wore. The women sometimes wore knickerbockers. The knickerbockers came down to their boot tops. Their long skirts covered the knickerbockers.

Many women kept diaries on the trail. Sometimes they wrote about seeing landmarks. Wagon trails followed landmarks so travelers could find their way. On the Oregon

Trail, pioneers saw Chimney Rock in western Nebraska, and Independence Rock in Wyoming.

Chimney Rock, Nebraska.

The pioneers also saw many marked graves. One woman wrote of seeing 80 graves in one 100 mile (161 km) stretch. She wrote that these were new graves. Older graves were not as easy to see and count. She also wrote about other things she saw on her trip, including Native Americans, bison (commonly called buffalo), and prairie dogs.

Another woman wrote that the trip took her family six months and three days to complete. They lived in their wagon and had many troubles. However, she wrote that it was worth the time and trouble because they found a new home.

A pile of stones mark the grave of a pioneer who died along the Oregon Trail near Guernsey, Wyoming.

A family of settlers gathers outside their sod home in Nebraska, 1880.

BUILDING NEW HOMES

One of the first things women did when they went west was to start new homes. Supplies and labor were not readily available in the West. People had to build homes out of what was available. In many areas logs were too rare and expensive. Some homes were little more than tents, while others were sod houses, or simple dugouts. In places where wood was available, settlers often built shake cabins.

Pioneers nailed the shakes to a frame to build a shake cabin. Log homes were commonly built in the Northwest and other places where wood was available.

Trees were not commonly found on the Great Plains, so many families built sod houses. Sod is the top layer of ground, with grass and weeds and roots still in it. Large pieces of sod were cut from the ground and stacked on top of each other. Sod houses, or "soddies," were cool in the summer and warm in the winter. But sod houses leaked during rainstorms, and after a storm water could drip from the ceiling for days. During a dry spell, pieces of dirt often fell from the ceiling.

On the Great Plains settlers also lived in dugouts. Settlers simply dug out part of a hill, then stacked thick pieces of sod to make a front wall. If settlers found wood, they used it for a roof. If no wood was available, they used sod instead.

Settlers who moved to the Southwest learned to build adobe houses. Adobe homes were built out of bricks that were made from clay mixed with straw and dried in the sun.

Many frontier homes had only one room in which a family squeezed all of its belongings. Families ate, slept, and spent most of their free time in this one room.

The fireplace was the center of the frontier home. Fireplaces gave homes heat and light. Women cooked meals at fireplaces with one or two heavy iron kettles and a skillet. A Dutch oven for baking bread was also nice to have. The best fireplaces included a turnspit for cooking meat.

Bed frames were too big to bring west in the wagons. Families brought their mattresses instead. After a while, the mattresses had to be re-stuffed with buffalo hair, prairie grass, hair from horses' manes, or husks from various seeds and fruits.

On the Great Plains, pioneers used whatever wood they could find to build furniture. Women often set tables that were made of boards from their wagons, or sat on rocking chairs made from sugar barrels.

Women used newspapers and magazines for wallpaper in order to cover their shake or dirt walls. They usually put up three or four layers to help keep their homes warm. Neighbors spent many hours "reading the walls" of their friends' houses.

Many women disliked their frontier homes. Tents were hot in the summer and cold in the winter. Shake cabins were weak. The dirt walls in dugouts would sometimes cave in. Log cabins were difficult to build. Walls made of adobe bricks would crack and have to be repaired. Sod houses were dark. Most of them had dirt floors, and they were difficult to keep clean. Worst of all, they were too small.

Families usually lived in tents or dugouts when they first arrived in the West. They built better homes when they could afford it.

This sod home, like many, had a dirt floor.

A pioneer couple stand arm in arm together.

COURTING AND HITCHING UP

Many children who grew up on the frontier stayed there as adults. When they grew up, most wanted to get married and start families of their own. Before getting married, couples found time during their busy lives to date. On the frontier, a date was called something different than it is today. A young woman had a young man "keep her company," or "come to call." If he wanted to "spark," or kiss, she "gave him the mitten," or stopped seeing him, if she wasn't interested.

Farmers asked young people to help husk corn or peel apples. After the work, farmers had dances. Young pioneers also met at harvest celebrations, weddings, and bees. These events gave young people a chance to be together. A young couple did different things on a date. They walked and talked, or picked berries. Sometimes they went to political or religious speeches, or danced, or sang to one another.

When a young couple was serious about each other, they courted. A courtship led to an engagement and marriage, or "getting hitched." Most women were around 18 years old when they were married.

When a pioneer man wanted to date a woman, he would "come to call." The date often involved little more than a pleasant stroll and chat.

People called honeymoons "bridal tours" and "wedding tours." Another name for a honeymoon was a "wedding journey." Many newlyweds spent their honeymoons traveling across the West to start their new lives. If a couple had enough money they might honeymoon in a big city.

Many people thought marriage was a woman's life calling, or job. Marriage meant happiness but also a lot of work. Women depended on their husbands for money. They took care of the children, sewed, cooked, cleaned, and helped out with the farming or ranching work. The women worked very hard.

A bride in her wedding dress, 1862.

WOMEN'S WORK

Frontier women fed, clothed, and took care of their husbands, children, and homes. A family with 6 to 12 children wasn't uncommon. Women had no sewing machine, washing machine, dryer, refrigerator, vacuum cleaner, or microwave oven. But they did have strength, endurance, and determination.

Most people lived far away from clothing stores, and "store bought" clothes cost a lot of money. Only a small number of people could afford to buy clothes. Instead, most frontier women made their family's clothes. Each piece of clothing took hours to sew.

Many women had spinning wheels, and they spun wool into yarn. They also reused the good pieces of wool from worn out clothing. With these, they made coats, dresses, and stockings.

A woman holding pans of bread wears clothing typical of pioneers of the late nineteenth century.

Washing clothes was another duty that took hours to accomplish. Women scrubbed clothes on a washboard with homemade soap. They called the time they did laundry "washday," because it took a whole day's work to wash a family's clothes.

Women made laundry and bathing soap by putting cool ashes from a fireplace in a kettle of water, then boiling it. Boiling the water changed the ashes into liquid lye. (Lye is the ingredient in soap that takes dirt out of clothes.) Then she would dip lye from the first kettle into another kettle and stir the mixture until the liquid lye became a crusty foam.

Then, the kettle was emptied into a washtub. In a while, the foam went to the bottom of the washtub. The foam was now soap. Women generally made a two or three month's supply of soap. To make soap last longer, they added grease to the liquid lye and kept the soap in a dry place.

A settler scrubs clothing using a sudsy washboard.

Beef was hung beneath the canopy of a covered wagon in order to dry.

Preserving food also took a lot of time. Women cut meat into strips. They placed the strips in the sun, which dried the meat so that it kept for a long time. Women also salted the strips. They would hang the heavily salted strips by the fireplace, and the heat would dry the meat. On the trail, meat was hung in the wagon to dry.

Fixing a meal was tiring work. Women needed good water and fuel to cook with. Some areas had alkali water. To make it usable, the women boiled it. Sometimes they boiled and flavored the water to make it taste better.

Cooking fires had to stay hot, so women constantly added wood. At the same time, they had to put food in kettles and hang them over the fire. During the time the food cooked, women placed more wood in the fire. Three times each day women cooked for their families.

Most pioneer homes had kerosene lamps. However, kerosene cost money. To save money, many women made candles out of lard, or fat.

Taking care of sick children was another part of a frontier woman's life. Women placed mustard plasters on sick children's chests and made them drink tea and castor oil. For bleeding wounds, women placed either cobwebs or flour and salt on a cloth and then tied the cloth on the wound. For aching ears, they heated onions in tobacco leaves, then squeezed the juice from the heated mixture into the ear.

Women and men believed that the best remedy for sickness was alcohol. They thought drinking or gargling an alcohol and salt mixture was a good treatment for colds. They poured alcohol on snakebites. Alcohol and peppermint oil were used to soothe burns.

As homemakers women had many other duties, too. They planted and took care of vegetable gardens. They tried to keep rattlesnakes, scorpions, and other unwelcome guests from their homes. Often they helped the men plant crops, tend them, and harvest them. Women on the frontier were always busy.

Central Pacific Railroad

Promontory
Point

Union Pacific Ra

Great
Salt Lake

Sacramento

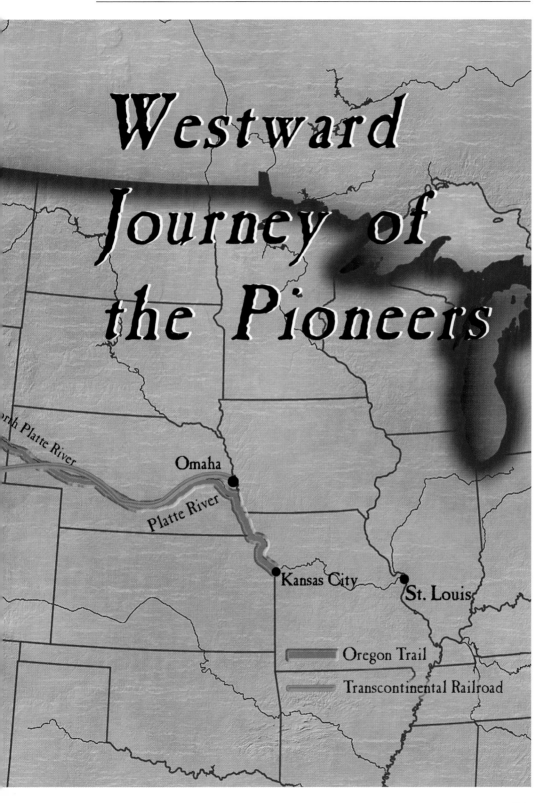

Westward Journey of the Pioneers

North Platte River

Omaha

Platte River

Kansas City

St. Louis

Oregon Trail

Transcontinental Railroad

READING, SOCIALS, AND SHIVAREES

Surviving on the frontier required a lot of hard work, but pioneers made time for fun, too. Pioneers read a lot of books, magazines, newspapers, and mail order catalogues in their free time.

Men generally read dime novels. These books had stories about explorers, hunters, and outlaws. The first dime novel sold hundreds of thousands of copies.

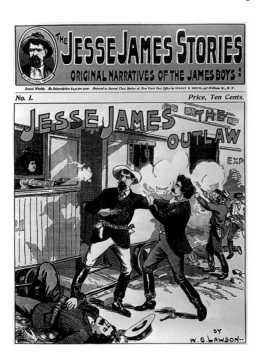

This dime novel was about the exploits of the Jesse James gang.

Women usually read different kinds of novels. They read books such as *Hard Cash*, *The Grey Woman*, and *Hyperion*. Women and men also read the Bible.

Many women signed up to receive magazines through the mail. They read *Ladies Home Journal*, *Godey's Lady's Book*, and *Harper's Bazaar.* They read weekly editions of the *New York Herald* and *New York World*.

Since women were busy and did not have much free time, they had few chances to wear their best dresses. Women could wear their best dresses to church services or dances. Dances were a favorite way to spend free time.

One or more fiddlers played at most dances. Sometimes other musicians played banjos, accordions, harmonicas, or guitars. Often another musician kept time on a mouth harp.

During the mid-1800s, Stephen Foster wrote many popular songs. He wrote the songs "Camptown Races," "My Old Kentucky Home," and "Oh! Susanna!" Other well-liked songs were "Dixie," "The Battle Hymn of the Republic," and "Lorena." Couples danced the polka, waltz, square dance, and quadrille. They danced on wooden floors, rough puncheon, or hard-packed dirt.

Saturday night socials were another way to spend free time. Neighbors came to one house for a Saturday night social. Adults talked about crops, community news, or books they had read. After the children went to sleep, the women sewed or crocheted. Often, Saturday night socials lasted until midnight or later.

Almost every pioneer wedding had a shivaree, or charivari, which was a noisy serenade to a newly married couple. In some areas people dressed up, painted their faces dark, or wore masks. They went to the newlywed couple's home, banging spoons against pots and kettles, or firing guns into the air. They made noise until the couple asked the group to come into their house. The couple then fed the group.

Living on the frontier included a lot of hard work. Women learned to adapt to the West and created better lives for themselves and their families.

A woodcut of a country dance held in 1883.

OPPORTUNITY ON THE FRONTIER

Although many women found life on the frontier to be harsh and untamed, some found the new land to be filled with opportunities. Western laws were among the first to allow women to own land and businesses, and in the Wyoming Territory women were allowed to vote.

In 1869, the Wyoming legislature decided that women should be free to vote in elections. Many people thought the Governor John Campbell would never let the law pass. However, the governor agreed with the legislature, and he signed the bill allowing Wyoming women to vote. They were the first women voters in the world.

The right to vote was only one of the reasons women traveled thousands of miles through harsh conditions. Women also came to the West for the same reasons men did: free land. Many women started their own cattle ranches or farms. Many were anxious for the excitement and fulfillment of owning and working their own land.

The majority of women came to the frontier with their husbands. Pioneers who were new to the frontier learned quickly that it took more than one person to maintain a ranch or farm in the uncivilized western land. This meant that husbands depended on their wives not only to cook, clean, and raise children, but also to haul water, chop wood, fix broken fences, herd farm animals, and hunt for food. Many women worked side by side with men. Wives and daughters often maintained their farms while their husbands and fathers were gone on cattle drives. The rigid boundaries of men and women's work didn't apply on the frontier.

A woman named Lizzie Williams ran her cattle operation separately from her husband's. She prospered while her husband Hezekiah often went into debt. Lizzie became one of the most successful cattle dealers in Texas.

Some women who were born on the frontier grew up listening to their fathers' tales of wild adventures as cowboys, and wanted a taste of it themselves. Women could find jobs as cowgirls, but those hiring them often questioned their ability to ride horses and herd cattle. Sometimes women dressed in men's clothing to be hired.

A widow named Mrs. E.J. Guerin, also called Mountain Charley, dressed as a man for 13 years. She worked on railways and herded cattle in order to earn money to support her children. For women on the frontier, survival meant doing whatever was necessary.

INTERNET SITES

http://www.wsu.edu:8080/~harvill/

This well-constructed Web site shows how, unlike the stereotype of women, pioneer women were strong and resilient. The roles of women in the early American West are examined. The site also provides a very interesting look at the author's family and experiences as pioneers in the Northwest United States.

http://lcweb2.loc.gov/ammem/award97/ndfahtml/hult_women.html

Part of the Fred Hultstrand History in Pictures Collection of the Library of Congress, this site provides a glimpse of pioneer women performing chores, wearing fashions of the day, in social settings, and operating their own businesses.

These sites are subject to change. Go to your favorite search engine and type in "women pioneers" for more sites.

PASS IT ON

History buffs: educate readers around the country by passing on information you've learned about early-American women pioneers. Share your little-known facts and interesting stories. We want to hear from you! To get posted on the ABDO Publishing Company Web site, email us at "History@abdopub.com"

Visit the ABDO Publishing Company Web site at:
www.abdopub.com

GLOSSARY

Alkali: A kind of water that has salt in it and is harsh on the skin.

Bee: A group of people gathering to work on something special, such as building a township hall, or making quilts.

Boarding house: A place where people could rent rooms and eat meals.

Buffalo chips: Dried buffalo manure.

Calico: A heavy, plain cotton cloth.

Cholera: A disease that causes vomiting, diarrhea, and stomach cramps. It often kills the infected person.

Conestoga wagon: A strong, well-made wagon used for traveling long distances.

Dime novels: Short, exciting novels that cost a dime.

Dugouts: Shelters dug into the sides of hills.

Dutch oven: An iron kettle with a tight cover used for baking bread on a fireplace.

Fiddle: A violin.

Great Plains: The land from the Rocky Mountains to just west of the Mississippi River, and from the Rio Grande to the delta of the MacKenzie River in Canada.

Mouth harp: A metal instrument held between the lips and hit by a finger to make music.

Knickerbockers: Short, loose-fitting pants worn by pioneer women.

Legislature: A group of people who make laws.

Puncheon: Split logs tied together.

Shakes: Pieces of logs that are split and cut into short lengths.

Smallpox: A disease that causes high fever and open sores.

Sod house: A house made from dirt and grass. Also called soddies.

Turnspit: A thin rod that holds meat over a fireplace.

Wagon train: A group of travelers heading west in covered wagons.

INDEX

Raggedy Ann and Andy Go Flying

By Mary Fulton

Illustrated by Judith Hunt

BASED ON THE CHARACTERS CREATED BY JOHNNY GRUELLE

GOLDEN PRESS · NEW YORK
Western Publishing Company, Inc., Racine, Wisconsin

What excitement in the playroom — Marcella had been
packing all morning. "I wish I could take you all with me,"
she told the dolls, hurrying to close her suitcase. "This is my
first trip on an airplane. It's going to be such fun flying!"

Raggedy Ann and Andy were neatly tucked in their beds.

"Be good while I'm at Grandma's," Marcella told them,
"and take care of the other dolls for me. When I get back next
week, I'll tell you all about my flight."

Raggedy Ann and Andy just smiled, for dolls don't talk to people.

But as soon as Marcella slammed the front door, Raggedy Ann popped out of bed. "I wish I could go flying, too!" she cried.

"So do I!" shouted Raggedy Andy, jumping out of bed.

"*Ruff-ruff,*" barked Raggedy Arthur.

"I would love to zoom up
in a plane," said Ann.

"I would love to fly like
a bird," said Andy.

Suddenly Ann stopped pretending to fly, ran to
the window, and looked out. "I've got it!" she cried.
"We *can* go flying! Come on, Andy, follow me!"

Raggedy Andy and Raggedy
Arthur couldn't imagine what
Ann was thinking of.
But they followed
her as she raced
down the
stairs . . .

. . . out the door . . .

. . . across the yard,
and down to the pond.

A big white goose was swimming in the pond.
Ann politely asked him if he would take them flying.

"No one can fly higher or faster than I can," boasted
the goose. "I'll be glad to take you."

"Hooray!" cried Ann and Andy together.

Raggedy Arthur just shook his head and growled.
He didn't want any part of flying.

"Let's go!" shouted Andy, and
he hopped aboard the goose's back.
"Wait for me!" exclaimed
Raggedy Ann, grabbing Andy's hand.
"Hold on tight!" honked the goose.
He took a few running steps,
flapped his wings, and
left the ground.

"*Ruff-ruff-ruff,*" barked Raggedy Arthur frantically
as the goose soared into the sky, carrying his friends.

Raggedy Ann and Andy watched as
Marcella's house got smaller and smaller. The
pond became just a tiny patch of blue. Raggedy
Arthur, a little speck of yellow, was running
round and round in circles.

"Look, Andy," cried Ann. "Isn't it beautiful?"

"Whoopee!" yelled Andy. "We're flying!
We're really flying!"

"Flying!" honked the goose.
"You call this flying?" With that
he raised one wing overhead and
went into a dive.

"Oh, my goodness!" cried Andy,
grabbing his hat.

"Oh!" gasped Ann as the pond
got closer and closer.

Suddenly Ann
found herself face to
face with a fish.

But before she could even say hello,
the goose was up and away again.

"Now you're really going to see something,"
said the goose, and he began to swoop and soar like
a roller-coaster. He had forgotten his passengers.
"Hang on, Ann!" shouted Andy.
"I'm trying, Andy," cried Raggedy Ann.

Suddenly the goose
turned a loop-the-loop and
Ann and Andy fell off.

"Help, help!" cried
Raggedy Ann, flapping her
arms as she fell toward the
ground.

Then her skirt billowed
up around her face and she
realized it was almost as
good as a parachute. She
looked around for Andy. He
was using his hat to catch
the wind and slow his fall.

"Oof," said Andy, thumping onto the ground.

"Whoof," said Ann, as she landed on something soft.

"*Ruff-ruff,*" said Raggedy Arthur, because he was the something soft Raggedy Ann had landed on.

"It's a good thing we're made of cotton," said Ann when she saw that Andy and Arthur were all right.

"Look at that," Ann said,
as Andy helped her up.
"We've landed in our yard."
"Good," said Andy.
"I certainly don't feel like
walking home after what
we've just been through."

Then, with wobbly knees, the three
Raggedys made their way back
to Marcella's playroom.

When Marcella came back from her trip,
the dolls were neatly tucked in their beds, just as she
had left them a week earlier.

"I'm so glad to be home," she said, hugging Ann and Andy.

"My goodness, you're all lumpy!" she exclaimed.

"How in the world did your stuffing get so bunched up?"